CLOSE-UP

OUR HOMES

BROWN
BEAR
BOOKS

Published by Brown Bear Books Limited

An imprint of
The Brown Reference Group plc
68 Topstone Road
Redding
Connecticut
06896
USA
www.brownreference.com

ISBN: 978-1-93383-415-3

Authors: John Woodward and Leon Gray
Designer: Lynne Lennon
Picture Researcher: Rupert Palmer
Managing Editor: Bridget Giles
Production Director: Alastair Gourlay
Children's Publisher: Anne O'Daly

Picture credits
Front cover: Science Photo Library: Eye of Science
Title page: Science Photo Library: Andrew Syred
Science Photo Library: 7, 9, 29, Dr. Tony Brain & David Parker 5, Dr. Jeremy Burgess 11, 13, Eye of Science 21, Steve Gschmeissner 19, David Scharf 27, Andrew Syred 15, 17, 23, 25.

Library of Congress Cataloging-in-Publication Data

Our homes.

    p. cm. – (Close-up)

  Includes bibliographical references and index.

  ISBN-13: 978-1-933834-15-3 (alk. paper)

  1. Household supplies–Juvenile literature. 2. Home economics–Equipment and supplies–Juvenile literature. I. Title. II. Series.

  TX148.O87 2007

  640–dc22

2006103051

Printed in China
9 8 7 6 5 4 3 2 1

Contents

Harm and Help

Tiny creatures called bacteria live all around us. They are in our food, in the air, and in the water we drink. Some bacteria live on plants. Others live on and inside animals, including people. Bacteria are so small we can only see them using microscopes.

Killer Bacteria

Some bacteria produce chemicals that kill other bacteria. Scientists use these chemicals to make drugs called antibiotics. Penicillin is an antibiotic. Doctors use antibiotics to help ill people get better. The antibiotics kill the harmful bacteria inside the sick person's body.

Good and bad

Some bacteria are harmful to people. They grow inside our bodies or in our food and make us feel ill. Other types of bacteria are helpful to people. People use some bacteria to make food such as cheese and yogurt. Other bacteria are used to make drugs that cure diseases.

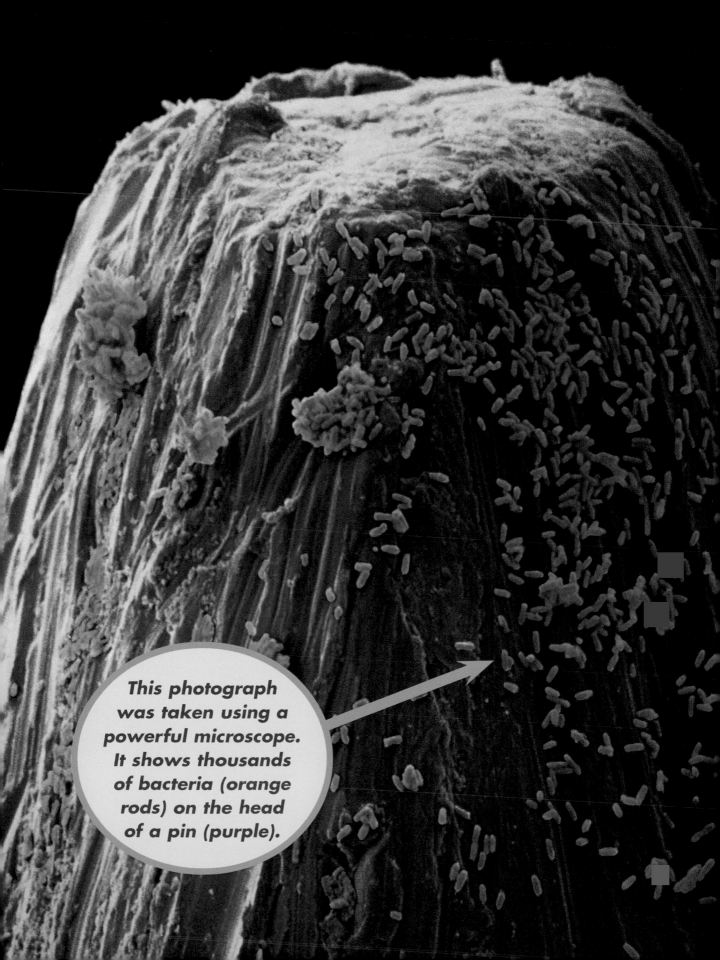

Plastic Foam

Many objects in the home contain plastic. Plastic does not occur in nature. It is synthetic, which means it is made by people. Polyurethane is one type of plastic. It can be made into a plastic foam.

Soft and hard

Polyurethane foam can be soft or hard. Soft polyurethane foam is easy to squeeze, like a sponge. It is used to stuff cushions and pillows. Hard polyurethane foam is strong and light. It is used to make the insides of an airplane's wings.

Limited Reserves

Plastic is synthetic, but it is made from natural materials. Most plastics are made using petroleum. Petroleum is the fuel that powers automobiles and airplanes. There is only a limited amount of petroleum on Earth. When all the petroleum is used up, there will be no more left to use.

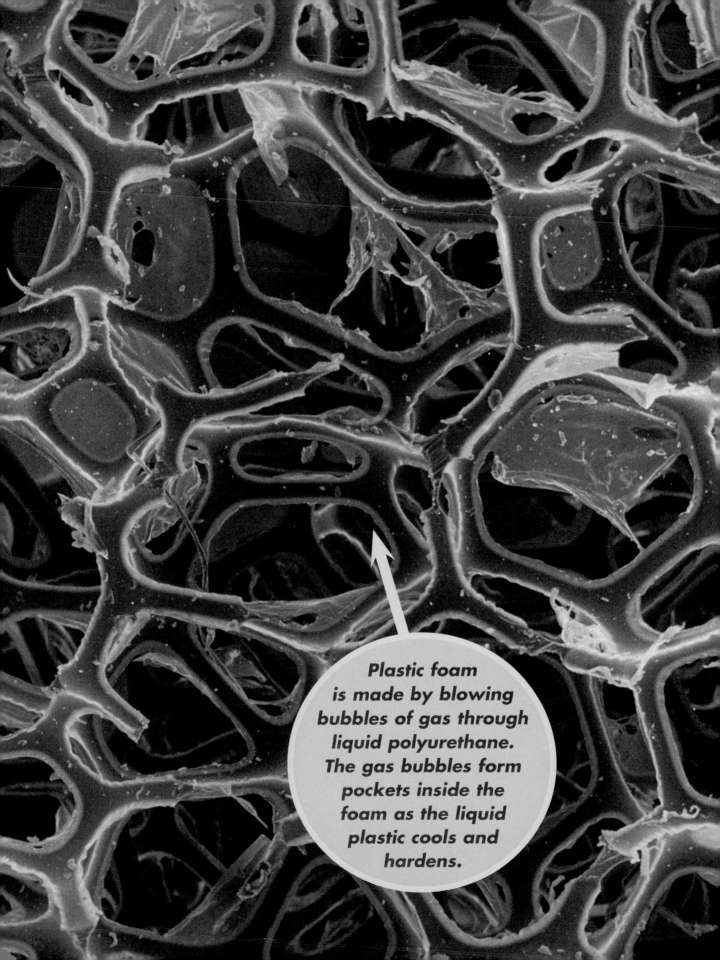

Plastic foam is made by blowing bubbles of gas through liquid polyurethane. The gas bubbles form pockets inside the foam as the liquid plastic cools and hardens.

Liquid Plastic

Polyester is a fiber made from liquid plastic. The liquid plastic is put into a container. The container is made to spin around at high speed. As it spins, the plastic squeezes through tiny holes in a machine called a spinneret. The plastic cools into long fibers called filaments.

Glass Fiber

German-born silkmaker Louis Schwabe (1798–1845) made the first glass fibers in 1842. He heated glass into liquid or molten glass. Then he forced the molten glass through tiny holes in a machine. When the molten glass appeared through the hole it cooled and hardened into long glass fibers.

Using polyester

Polyester filaments can be woven to make clothes and household items such as bedsheets and curtains. Polyester filaments are often mixed with natural fibers such as cotton. This makes polyester clothing more comfortable to wear.

Fibers of a polyester called Dacron are used to make the lining of a sleeping bag. Each fiber contains pockets of trapped air, which help to keep in heat.

Light into Sound

Compact discs (CDs) have been used to record and play music since 1982. Music is recorded onto a master disc using a laser. The laser burns tiny grooves onto the disc as it spins at high speed. The master is used to make CDs that people buy.

Playing CDs

When a CD is put in a CD player, a laser shines light at the CD. Light bounces off the grooves and is changed back into sound. Computers can also play and record information onto CDs.

Storing More

A CD can store about 75 minutes of music or 100 million words. A digital versatile disc (DVD) can store about seven times as much as a CD. Scientists are now developing new disks, such as Blu-ray discs and holographic video discs (HVDs), that can store much more.

Velcro Pioneer

Swiss scientist George de Mestral invented Velcro in 1948. Velcro is made from a plastic called nylon. It is made of two strips. Hooks on one strip link up with hoops on the other strip. The links form a strong bond. Velcro is often used instead of zippers or buttons to fasten clothes and bags.

Mighty Velcro

There are more than 2,800 hooks or 48,000 hoops on 1 square inch (6.5 cm²) of Velcro. The same piece of Velcro could support the weight of two adult men weighing 200 pounds (90 kg) each!

Inventing Velcro

De Mestral came up with his idea from the way burrs from plants stuck to his clothes. When he looked at the burrs under a microscope, he saw that they were covered in tiny hooks. De Mestral realized that the hooks were holding onto the fibers of his clothing.

One strip of Velcro is covered with tiny hooks. The other is covered with hoops. When you press the strips together, the hooks link through the hoops.

Easy Writer

Felt-tip pens are fun to use for drawing and writing on paper. The pens come in a range of different colors. A tube of thick ink is stored inside the pens, so the pens do not get messy.

Ink flow

One end of the ink tube is joined to a nib or tip made of felt. As you move the pen across a piece of paper, ink runs down the tube. It flows through the nib and onto the paper. The ink dries as soon as it touches the paper.

Fiber versus Felt

Pens with fiber tips have nibs made from fibers glued in a tight bundle. The nibs of fiber-tip pens come in different thicknesses. Fine nibs have fewer fibers than thick nibs. Fiber-tip pens last longer than felt-tip pens. The glued fiber nib also keeps its shape better than a felt nib.

Chemical Chips

Everything in the universe is made of elements. Most elements are metals, like copper and gold. But some are nonmetals, such as oxygen. Silicon is a chemical element. Silicon is unusual because it acts both like a metal and a nonmetal.

Downsizing

The first computers were so big, they filled entire rooms. Early computers struggled to do sums that you can do today using a pocket calculator. Silicon chips have made computers much smaller and more powerful. Modern silicon chips are no bigger than your fingernail.

Silicon chips

Silicon is very important. It is used to make parts for electronic machines. Electric circuits that control the machines are scratched onto the surface of wafer-thin slices of silicon, known as chips. Silicon chips are used in all electronic machines, from computers to space probes.

Seeing the Light

The glowing part of a lightbulb is called the filament. The filament is a thin wire that measures just a few hundredths of a millimeter thick. The wire is made from a metal called tungsten. The filament sits in the middle of a glass bulb.

Heat to light

When you flick a light switch on, electricity flows through the filament. The filament heats up and glows to light up the room. Over time, the heat weakens the filament. The lightbulb burns out.

Terrific Tungsten

When electricity flows through the filament of a lightbulb, the tungsten glows white hot. The tungsten reaches a temperature of 4,500°F (2,480°C). Even at such a high temperature, the tungsten does not melt. In fact, tungsten has the highest melting point of all the metals.

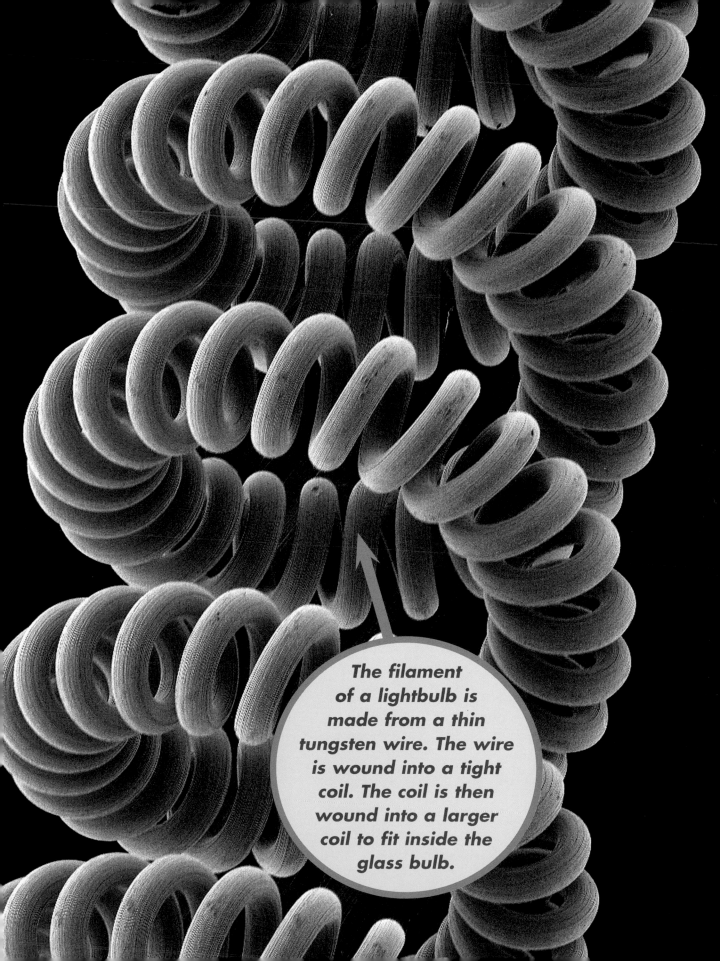

Bite the Dust

Every house contains millions and millions of dust mites. Mites are tiny animals with round bodies and eight legs. Although mites look like insects, they are close relatives of spiders, scorpions, and ticks. All these creatures belong to a group called the arachnids.

Mite Parasite

Mites make their homes in many places. Some live in the soil or in water. Others live on the bodies of other animals. Some mites live in the ears of moths. Others live on human skin. Many mites are harmless, but some cause diseases. Mites that harm the animals they live on are called parasites.

Sharing a bed

Dust mites live everywhere that dust is found—on carpets, curtains, and furniture. In fact, every time you go to bed you share it with about two million dust mites. Dust mites feed on flakes of dead skin and other bits and pieces that make up household dust.

Devilish Dust

Household dust is a mix of plant and animal parts. Humans create most of the dust. People shed dead skin cells and lose hairs from their head. Pet hair, insect droppings, and parts of plants such as pollen grains are also in dust.

Dust allergy

Some people get itchy skin and sore eyes when they come into contact with household dust. This is known as a dust allergy. In some cases, the allergy can lead to a breathing condition called asthma.

Hairy Situation

Household dust contains a lot of hair. An adult has about 100,000 hairs on his or her head. Every day, between 20 and 100 hairs fall to the ground as dust. The fur from our pets and unwelcome guests such as mice add to this dust.

Dust contains many tiny objects. Human hair, skin cells, and fibers from our clothes, as well as animal fur, insect droppings, and pollen grains all make up dust.

Spinning a Yarn

Cotton is a natural fiber used to make cloth. It comes from the cotton plant. When the flowers of the cotton plant die, round seed cases called cotton bolls replace them. When the cotton bolls are ripe, they burst open. Inside each boll is a ball of fluffy, creamy cotton. The cotton protects seeds tucked inside the boll.

Cotton Belt

Much of the world's cotton comes from the United States. Cotton is grown over a huge area, from Florida north to North Carolina and west to California. This area is known as the Cotton Belt. Cotton has a long history in the Americas. Pieces of cotton dating back 7,000 years have been found in Mexico.

Cotton to cloth

Cotton from the boll is washed and then pulled into long fibers. Fibers are spun into yarns by twisting them together into one long strand of cotton. The cotton yarns are ready to be woven into cloth.

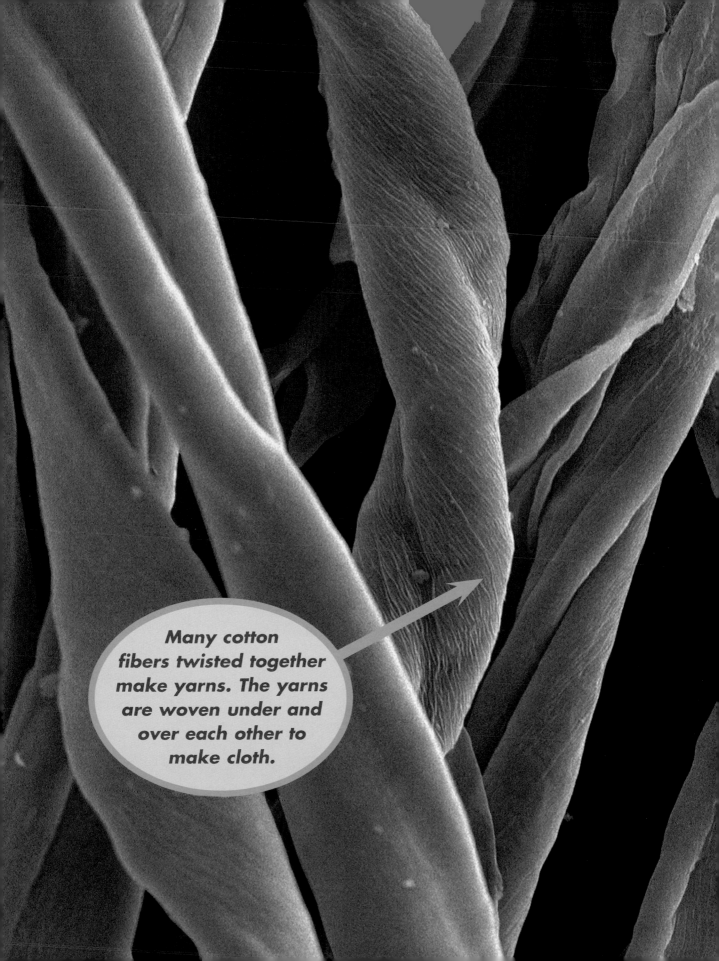

House Haunters

Cockroaches live all over the world. Most live in houses and other places where people are. Cockroaches are pests because they eat our food and spread diseases. It is hard to stop cockroaches because they are quick and can hide in tiny cracks.

American cockroach

The American cockroach is a regular cockroach. It grows up to 1.5 inches (4 centimeters) long. It is mainly active at night, when it searches for scraps of food left by its human hosts.

Old Insects

Cockroaches are some of Earth's oldest insects. The remains of dead cockroaches have been found locked away inside rocks. These remains are called fossils. Scientists think that the fossils may be 300 million years old or more.

To the Rescue

A Band-Aid is a key part of any first-aid kit. It is used to cover a minor wound. A pad on the underside of the Band-Aid protects the wound from more harm. The pad also soaks up blood from the wound. A slippery coating on the surface of the pad stops the pad from sticking to the wound.

Band-Aid

A Band-Aid should only be used on minor cuts and grazes. The wound should be cleaned with water before the Band-Aid is used. Dirt in the wound may cause disease. Never use Band-Aids on a burn because they may stick to burned skin.

Sticky bandage

The Band-Aid has a sticky surface to keep the pad firmly pressed to the skin. When the Band-Aid is taken off, the sticky surface peels away from the skin. Tiny holes in the Band-Aid let air through to the wound, helping it to heal.

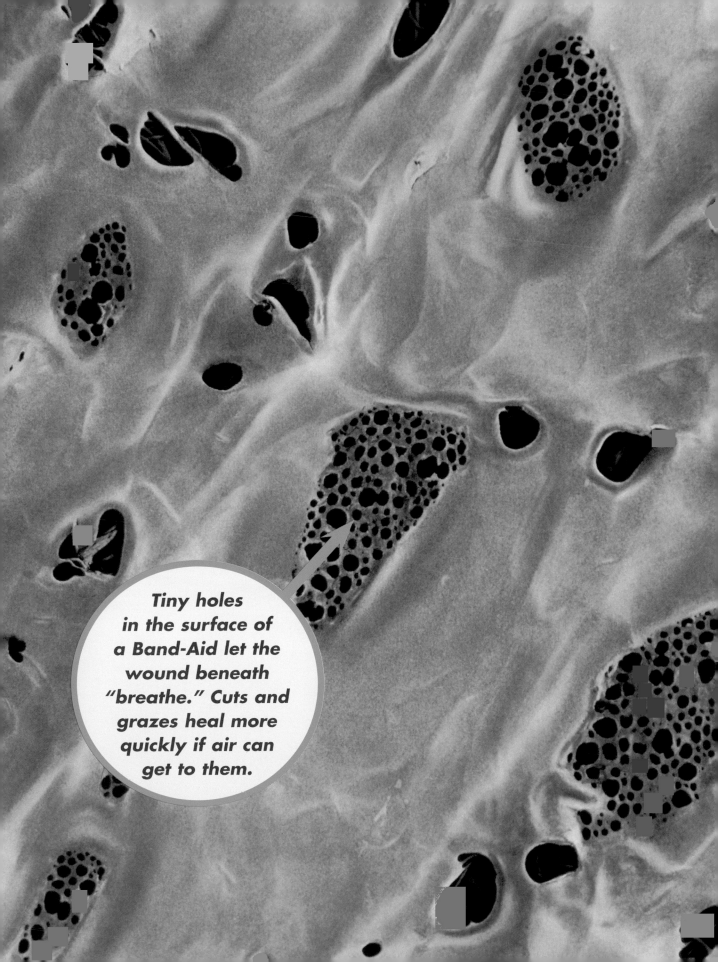

Glossary

allergy: the body's response to harmless substances such as dust, pollen, and certain foods.

antibiotic: any drug that destroys bacteria and other harmful germs.

bacteria: tiny, single-celled creatures that can be helpful or harmful to people.

disease: something that stops the body of a living creature from working properly.

electricity: a form of energy that people use to light buildings and power machines.

element: a pure substance that cannot be broken down into other substances.

fiber: a thin thread of material such as cotton, glass, or wool.

laser: a machine that makes a narrow beam of powerful light.

parasite: a living creature that lives and feeds on another living creature and causes it harm.

plastic: a synthetic material with many uses.

pollen: small, yellow grains that are the male parts of a flower.

spinneret: a machine that forces liquids through holes to make long filaments.

synthetic: something that is made by people.

Further Study

Books

Gifford, Clive. *Materials (Kingfisher Young Knowledge)*. New York: Kingfisher, 2005.

Gordon, Sharon. *Allergies (Rookie Read-About Science)*. New York: Children's Press, 2003.

Green, Emily K. *Cockroaches (Blastoff! Readers/World of Insects)*. Eden Prairie, Minnesota: Bellwether Media (in conjunction with Scholastic), 2006.

Snedden, Robert. *Yuck!: A Big Book of Little Horrors*. New York: Simon & Schuster Children's Publishing, 1996.

Trumbauer, Lisa. *Tiny Life in Your Home (Rookie Read-About Science)*. New York: Children's Press, 2006.

Web sites

www.pestworldforkids.org
Explore the world of pests that might live in your home and backyard. Play fun games as you learn about pests.

teachingplastics.org/hop_jr/activities/index.html
This web page contains a list of fun games and activities to help you learn more about plastics and their impact on everyday life.

Index